ELGAR

The Kingdom

OPUS 51

an oratorio for soprano, alto, tenor & bass soli, SATB & orchestra

Order No: NOV 070106R

NOVELLO PUBLISHING LIMITED
8/9 Frith Street, London W1V 5TZ

FULL SCORE AND ORCHESTRAL MATERIAL
AVAILABLE ON HIRE

A. M. D. G.

Plas Gwyn,
1905-6.

The sign R - - - ⌐ signifies *ritardando*.

  „ „ A - - - ⌐   „   *accelerando*.

  „ „ L - - - ⌐   „   *largamente*.

THE KINGDOM

JERUSALEM

PRELUDE.

I.—IN THE UPPER ROOM.

The Disciples and the Holy Women.

Seek first the Kingdom of God.
and His righteousness.

Peter.

Peace be multiplied unto you.

The Disciples and the Holy Women.

Peace;
peace be unto thee,
and peace be to thine helpers.

———

Peter.

" Where two or three are gathered together in
My Name,
there am I in the midst of them."

Mary, Mary Magdalene, John and Peter.

Remember the words of the Lord Jesus,—

The Disciples and the Holy Women.

Jesus, the Holy One.

John.

" Surely they are My people ':

The Disciples and the Holy Women.

so He was their Saviour ;

Mary.

For while all things were in quiet silence,
and that night was in the midst of her swift
course,
Thine almighty Word leaped down from heaven
out of Thy royal throne.

The Disciples and the Holy Women

The Light of the world.

Mary Magdalene.

The Dayspring from on high hath visited us,
to guide our feet into the way of peace.

The Disciples and the Holy Women.

The Way,
the Truth,
and the Life.

John.

Did not their heart burn within them,
while He talked with them by the way ?

Peter.

He took bread,
and blessed it,
and brake,
and gave it to us.

The Disciples and the Holy Women.

The true Vine ;
the Bread of Life.

All.

Let them give thanks
whom the Lord hath redeemed ;
He remembered His holy promise.

In the concord of brethren,
in the love of neighbours,
O praise the Name of the Lord our God.

The true Vine,
The Bread of Life :
He brake,
and gave It to us.

Praise the Name of our God,
That hath dealt wondrously with us.

Amen.

———

Peter.

Men and brethren :
it was needful that the scripture should be
fulfilled, which the Holy Ghost spake before
by the mouth of David concerning Judas,
who was guide to them that took Jesus : for
he was numbered among us, and had
obtained part of this ministry.

The Disciples and the Holy Women.

" Let his habitation be desolate,
   and let no man dwell therein,
   and let his office let another take."

Peter.

Wherefore of these men which have companied
   with us all the time that the Lord Jesus
   went in and out among us, must one be
   ordained to be a witness with us of His
   resurrection.

Peter, John and the Disciples.

Thou, Lord,
   Which knowest the hearts of all men,
   shew of these two
   the one whom Thou hast chosen,
   to take the place in this ministry
   and apostleship.

———

CHORAL RECITATIVE.

They gave forth their lots :
   (The lot is cast ;
   but the whole disposing thereof
   is of the Lord).
and the lot fell upon Matthias ;
   and he was numbered
   with the eleven Apostles.

*John, Peter, Mary, Mary Magdalene, the Disciples
and the Holy Women.*

The Lord hath chosen you
   to stand before Him to serve Him ;
   you shall be named the Priest of the Lord.

———

CHORUS.

O ye priests !
   Seemeth it but a small thing
   that God hath separated you
   to bring you near to Himself,
   to stand before the congregation
   to minister unto them ?
For it is not ye that speak,
   but the Spirit of your Father
   Which speaketh in you :
the Lord hath chosen you ;
   ye are the messengers
   of the Lord of hosts.
It is not ye that speak,
   but the Spirit of your Father
   Which speaketh in you.
O ye priests !
   This commandment is for you.

———

II.—AT THE BEAUTIFUL GATE.

THE MORN OF PENTECOST.

Mary and Mary Magdalene.

The singers are before the altar ;
   they make sweet melody,
   and sing the words of David,
   the sweet psalmist ;
     he beautified the feasts
     that the temple might sound from morning.

The Lord hath prepared a sacrifice ;
   the day of the First-Fruits.

———

This man, lame from his mother's womb,
   is carried daily to the Beautiful Gate ;

To him that is afflicted pity should be shewed ;
   let us give alms of such things as we have.

———

The blind and the lame came to Jesus
   in the temple,
     and He healed them,

He knew their sorrows ;
   Himself took their infirmities,
   and bare their sicknesses.

He hath looked down from the
   height of His sanctuary,
     to hear their sighing.

———

The service of the Lord is prepared ;
   the day of the First-Fruits :

   let us go into the house of the Lord.

———

III.—PENTECOST.

IN THE UPPER ROOM.

RECITATIVE. (TENOR.)

And when the day of Pentecost was fully come,
   they were all with one accord in one place.

———

The Disciples.

When the great Lord will,
   we shall be filled
   with the Spirit of understanding.

MYSTIC CHORUS (SOPRANOS AND CONTRALTOS).

The Spirit of the Lord shall rest upon them;
 the spirit of wisdom and understanding.
 the spirit of counsel and might,
 the spirit of knowledge.
Come from the four winds,
 O Spirit !

 " I will pour forth of My Spirit,
  and they shall prophesy ;
  and I will shew wonders
  in the heaven above,
  and signs on the earth beneath."

John.

When the Comforter is come,
 we shall bear witness ;

Peter.

and speak as moved
 by the Holy Spirit.

The Disciples.

When the great Lord will,
 we shall be filled
 with the Spirit of understanding.

———

RECITATIVE. (CONTRALTO.)

And suddenly there came from heaven a sound
 as of the rushing of a mighty wind, and it
 filled all the house where they were sitting ;
 and there appeared unto them tongues
 parting asunder, like as of fire ; and it
 sat upon each one of them :—

And they were all filled with the Holy Spirit,
 and began to speak with other tongues,
 as the Spirit gave them utterance.

The Disciples.

He, Who walketh upon the wings of the wind,
 shall baptize with the Holy Ghost.
 and with fire,
He, Whose ministers are flaming fire,
 shall baptize with the Holy Ghost,
 and with fire.

MYSTIC CHORUS. (SOPRANOS AND ALTOS.)

 (The Lord put forth His hand,
  and touched their mouth ;
 God hath spoken,
  who can but prophesy ?)

RECITATIVE. (CONTRALTO.)

And there were dwelling in Jerusalem Jews,
 devout men, from every nation under
 heaven ; and when this sound was heard,
 the multitude came together, and were all
 amazed, and marvelled.

———

IN SOLOMON'S PORCH.

The People.

Behold, are not all these which speak,
 Galilæans ?
And how hear we, every man in our tongue,
 wherein we were born ?

John.

He, Who walketh upon the wings of the wind,
 hath baptized with the Holy Ghost,
 and with fire.

The People.

We do hear them speak in our tongues the
 wonderful works of God !

Peter.

He, Whose ministers are flaming fire,
 hath baptized with the Holy Ghost,
 and with fire.

The People.
 What meaneth this ?

These men are full of new wine.

  They are truly full of power,
   even the Spirit of the Lord.

They drink, and forget the law, and pervert the
 judgment.

  With stammering lips
  and another tongue
  will He speak to this people.

When they heard, they trembled ;
 like men whom wine hath overcome, their
 lips quiver.

  Because of the Lord,
  and because of the words of His
  holiness.

We hear them speak in our tongues ;
 what meaneth this ?

Peter.

(" I have prayed for thee, that thy faith fail
 not ; and thou, when thou art converted,
 strengthen thy brethren.")

———

Ye men of Judæa,
 and all ye that dwell at Jerusalem,
 be this known unto you,
 and give ear unto my words :

This is that which was spoken by the Prophet,—
 " It shall come to pass in the last days,
  saith God,
 I will pour forth of My Spirit upon all flesh:
 and your sons and your daughters shall
  prophesy,
 and your young men shall see visions,
 and your old men shall dream dreams ;
 and it shall be that whosoever shall call on
  the Name of the Lord shall be saved."

Ye men of Israel, hear these words :

Jesus of Nazareth,
 a Man approved of God unto you
 by mighty works, and wonders, and signs,
 which God did by Him in the midst of you,
  as ye yourselves also know ;

Him, being delivered up by the determinate
 counsel and foreknowledge of God,
 ye, by the hand of lawless men
 did crucify and slay :

this Jesus hath God raised up,
 whereof we are all witnesses.

CHORUS. (SOPRANOS AND CONTRALTOS.)

(The Lord put forth His hand,
  and touched their mouth ;
 God hath spoken,
  who can but prophesy ?)

Peter.
Therefore,
 being exalted at the right hand of God,
 and having received of the Father
 the promise of the Holy Ghost,
He hath poured forth this,
 which ye now see and hear.

Let all the house of Israel know assuredly,
 that God hath made Him
 both Lord and Christ ;—

this Jesus Whom ye crucified.

The People.   (*Tenors and Basses.*)

(" His blood be on us,
  and on our children.")

Peter.

Whom ye crucified.

CONTRALTO. (SOLO.)

(" Daughters of Jerusalem,
  weep not for Me,
  but weep for yourselves,
  and for your children.")

The People.

Men and brethren, what shall we do ?

We have denied the Holy and Righteous One,
 and asked for a murderer to be granted to us ;
 we have killed the Prince of life.

Men and brethren, what shall we do ?

Peter.
Repent,—
 and be baptized every one of you,
in the Name of Jesus Christ ;
 for to you is the promise,
 and to your children,
 and to all that are afar off,
 even as many as the Lord our God
 shall call unto Him.

The People.

In the Name of Jesus Christ ;
 for to us is the promise,
 and to our children
 and to all that are afar off,
 even as many as the Lord our God
 shall call unto Him.

Pour upon us the Spirit of grace.

Peter.

In the Name of Jesus Christ.

The People.

Pour upon us the Spirit of grace.

All.

There shall be a fountain opened
 to the house of David.

In the Name of Jesus Christ :
 of His own will, God brought us forth
  by the word of truth, that we should be a
  kind of
 First-Fruits of His creatures,
in the Name of Jesus Christ,
 Whom the God of our fathers
 hath glorified.

IV.—THE SIGN OF HEALING.

AT THE BEAUTIFUL GATE.

RECITATIVE. (CONTRALTO.)

Then they that gladly received his word were
  baptized,
 and continued steadfastly in the Apostles'
  teaching,
 and in Fellowship,
  in the Breaking of Bread,
  and the Prayers ;
and fear came upon every soul, and many
 wonders and signs were done by the Apostles.

The man that was lame, at the Beautiful Gate, seeing Peter and John about to go into the temple, asked to receive an alms; and Peter, fastening his eyes upon him, with John, said :—

Peter.

Look on us.
Silver and gold have I none ;
  but what I have, that give I thee.
In the Name of Jesus Christ of Nazareth,
  rise up and walk.

The People.

This is he which sat for alms,
  lame from his mother's womb.
He entereth the temple,
  walking and praising God !

Peter.

Ye men of Israel,
  why marvel ye at this man ?
The God of Abraham, of Isaac, and of Jacob,
the God of our fathers
  hath glorified His Servant Jesus,
Whom ye delivered up :
by faith in His Name
  hath His Name made this man strong,
  whom ye behold and know.

John.

Unto you that fear His Name
  shall the Sun of righteousness arise
  with healing in His wings.
Unto you first God, having raised up His Servant, sent Him to bless you, in turning away every one of you from your iniquities.

Peter and John.

Turn ye again,
  that your sins may be blotted out,
  that so there may come seasons of refreshing
  from the presence of the Lord.

THE ARREST.

RECITATIVE. (CONTRALTO.)

And as they spake, the priests and the Sadducees came upon them, being sore troubled, because they proclaimed in Jesus the resurrection from the dead :
and they laid hands on them, and put them in ward unto the morrow;
  for it was now eventide.

Mary.

The sun goeth down ;
  Thou makest darkness,
  and it is night :
I commune with mine own heart,
  and meditate on Thee,
  in the night watches.
Blessed are ye when men shall persecute you for His sake.
  They deliver them up to the council,
  they are hated of men
    for His Name's sake ;
  all this is come upon them :—
  some shall they kill and crucify ;
Blessed are ye, reproached for the Name of Christ.
  Rejoice, ye partakers of His sufferings,
  that when His glory shall be revealed
  ye may be glad also,
  with exceeding joy.

How great are Thy signs,
  how mighty are Thy wonders ;
  Who healeth all infirmities.

The Gospel of the Kingdom
  shall be preached in the whole world ;
the Kingdom and patience,
  which are in Jesus.

The Branch of the Lord
  shall be beautiful and glorious.

Thou makest darkness,
  I meditate on Thee ;
in the night Thy song shall be with me
  a prayer unto the God of my life.

V.—THE UPPER ROOM.

IN FELLOWSHIP.

The Disciples and the Holy Women.

The voice of joy
  is in the dwelling of the righteous :
the stone which the builders rejected
  is become the head of the corner.

John.

The rulers asked :
  " By what power, or in what name, have ye done this ? "
Then Peter, filled with the Holy Spirit, said
  " In the Name of Jesus Christ."

The Disciples and the Holy Women.

In none other is there salvation :
  neither is there, under heaven,
  any other name
  wherein we must be saved.

Peter.

And when they took knowledge of us that we
had been with Jesus, they charged us not to
speak at all, nor teach in His Name;
we cannot but speak the things we saw and
heard.

John.

Finding nothing how they might punish us,
concerning a good deed done to an impotent
man, they further threatened us; and being
let go, we are come to our own company.

The Disciples and the Holy Women.

Lord, Thou didst make the heaven,
and the earth,
and the sea,
and all that in them is.
The rulers gather together
against the Lord and His Anointed:
Lord, behold their threatenings;
grant Thy servants to speak Thy word with
all boldness,
while Thou stretchest forth Thy hand to heal.
Praise the Name of our God
That hath dealt wondrously with us.

THE BREAKING OF BREAD.

The Disciples and the Holy Women.

Thou, Almighty Lord, hast given
food and drink to mankind;
but to us, Thou hast vouchsafed
spiritual food and drink
and life eternal
through Thy Servant.

Peter.

If any is holy;—

The Disciples.

let him come.

Peter.

If any is not;—

The Disciples and the Holy Women.

let him repent.

Mary, Mary Magdalene, John and Peter.
In the Name of Jesus Christ.

John.

Give thanks,—
first for the Cup.

The Disciples and the Holy Women.

We thank Thee, our Father,
for the Holy Vine.

Peter.

Give thanks,—
for the Broken Bread.

The Disciples and the Holy Women.

We thank Thee, our Father,
for the Life and Knowledge.
As this Broken Bread
was grain scattered upon the mountains,
and gathered together became one,
so may Thy Church be gathered together
from the bounds of the earth
into Thy Kingdom.

THE PRAYERS.

All.

Our Father,
Which art in Heaven,
hallowed be Thy Name;
Thy Kingdom come,
Thy will be done on earth
as it is in Heaven.
Give us this day our daily bread;
and forgive us our trespasses,
as we forgive them that trespass against us
and lead us not into temptation,
but deliver us from evil:
for Thine is the Kingdom,
the power,
and the glory;
for ever and ever,
Amen.

John.

Ye have received the Spirit of adoption,

Peter.

whereby we cry, Abba,—

Men.

Father.

All.

Thou, O Lord, art our Father,
our Redeemer,
and we are Thine.

THE BLESSED VIRGIN	...	...	...	...	*Soprano.*
MARY MAGDALENE	...	...	...	...	*Contralto.*
ST. JOHN	...	...	...	...	*Tenor.*
ST. PETER	...	...	...	...	*... Bass.*

JERUSALEM.

PRELUDE.

I.—IN THE UPPER ROOM.

THE KINGDOM.

JERUSALEM.

PRELUDE.

Edward Elgar, Op. 51.

12286

B

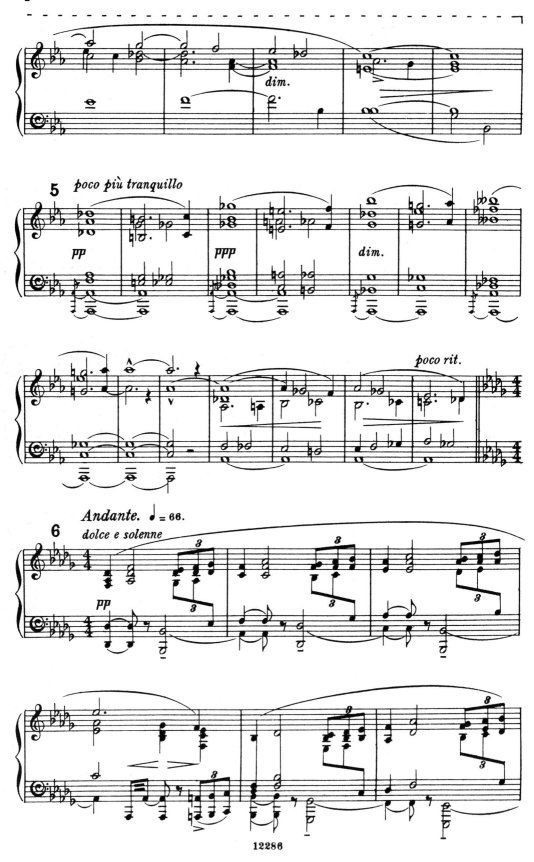

6

I.

IN THE UPPER ROOM.

THE DISCIPLES AND THE HOLY WOMEN.

* O sacrum Convivium.

were in quiet si-lence, and that night was in the midst of her swift

Sa-viour;

Sa-viour;

Sa-viour;

Sa-viour;

MARY MAGDALENE. *tranquillo*

The Day-spring from on high hath vis -- -it-ed us, to

dim. *pp*
of the world.

dim. *pp*
of the world.

dim. *pp*
of the world.

dim. *pp*
of the world.

tranquillo

dim. *pp*

23

dolce
guide our feet in-to the way of peace.

A _____

A _____

mf cresc.
The Way, ___ the

mf cresc.
The Way, ___ the

mf cresc.
The Way, ___ the

23

pp

mf

mf *cresc.*

cresc.

Ped. ✻ *Ped.* ✻

talked with them by the way?

molto più lento
PETER. *p solenne*

He took bread, and blessed it, and

brake, and gave it to us.

26 *a tempo*

The true Vine; The Bread of Life.

The true Vine; The Bread of Life.

The true Vine; The Bread of Life.

The true Vine; The Bread of Life.

CHORUS.

Let them give thanks whom the Lord hath re - deem - - ed:

Let them give thanks whom the Lord hath re - deem - - ed:

Let them give thanks whom the Lord hath re - deem - - ed:

Let them give thanks whom the Lord hath re - deem - - ed:

MARY.

He re-membered, He re-membered His ho-ly prom - - -

MARY MAGDALENE.

He re-membered, He re-membered His ho-ly prom - - -

JOHN.

He re-membered, He re-membered His ho-ly prom - -

PETER.

He re-membered, He re-membered His ho-ly prom - - -

SOLI.

24

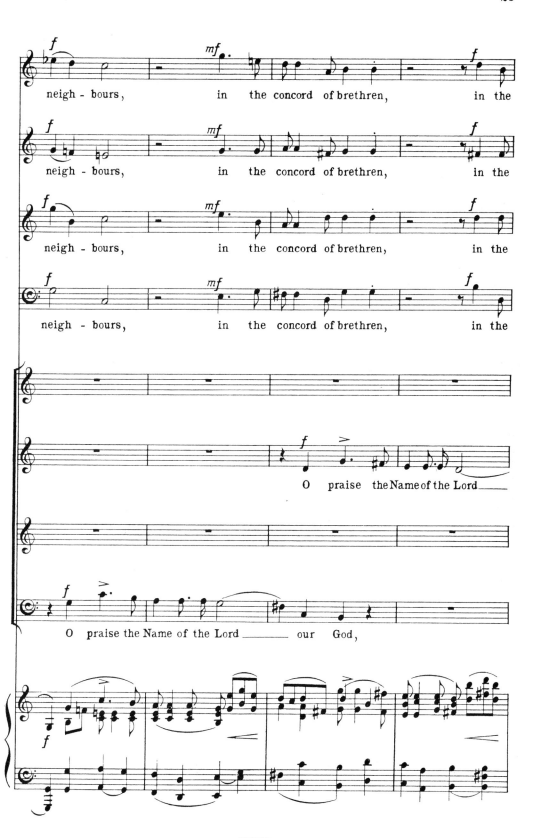

us, and had obtain-ed part of this min-is-try.

poco più lento

THE DISCIPLES and THE HOLY WOMEN.

CHORUS.

Soprano.
"Let his ha-bi-ta-tion be des - o-late, and let no man dwell there-

Alto.
"Let his ha-bi-ta-tion be des - o-late, and let no man dwell there-

Tenor.
"Let his ha-bi-ta-tion be des - o-late, and let no man dwell there-

Bass.
"Let his ha-bi-ta-tion be des - o-late, and let no man dwell there-

- in, and his of-fice let an - oth - - er

- in, and his of-fice let an - oth - - er

- in, and his of-fice let an - oth - - er

- in, and his of-fice let an - oth - - er

12286

40 molto L

cresc.

A

wit - ness with us of His res - ur -

(♩ = 80.)

p

cresc.

f

sf

A

- rec - tion.

A

ff

sf

Ped.

sf

Ped.

dim. molto

rit.

p

41 **Andante.**

THE DISCIPLES.

Tenor I.

p

Thou, Lord, Which knowest the hearts of all men,

Tenor II.

p

Thou, Lord, Which knowest the hearts of all men,

Bass I.

pp

Thou, Lord, Which knowest the hearts of all men,

Bass II.

p

Thou, Lord, Which knowest the hearts of all men,

CHORUS.

41 **Andante.** ♩ = 63.

pp

8va bassa

shew of these two the one whom Thou hast cho - sen,_____

shew of these two the one whom Thou hast cho - sen,_____

shew of these two the one whom Thou hast cho - sen,

shew of these two the one_____ whom Thou hast cho - sen,

_____ to take the place____ in this min-is-try and a - pos-tle - ship.____

to take the place____ in this min-is-try and a - pos-tle - ship.____

to take the place in this min-is-try and a - pos-tle - ship.____

to take the place in this min-is-try and a - pos-tle - ship.____

CHORUS.

48

12286

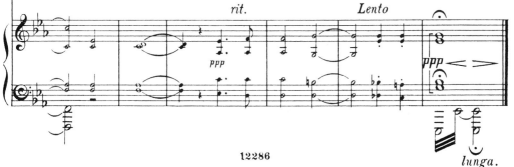

II.

AT THE BEAUTIFUL GATE.

(THE MORN OF PENTECOST).

sing-ers are be-fore the al - - tar; they make sweet me-lo-dy,

sick-ness-es.___ He hath look'd down from the height ___ of His sanctuary ___ to hear their sigh- -ing, to hear their sighing. ___

MARY MAGDALENE. The ser-vice of the Lord is pre-pared;

III.
PENTECOST.
IN THE UPPER ROOM.

MYSTIC CHORUS.

* Ten voices to each part until **73**.

F

When the great Lord will, we shall be fill - ed with the Spir-it of

When the great Lord will, we shall be filled with the Spir-it of

When the great Lord will, we shall be filled with the Spir-it of

When the great Lord will, we shall be fill - ed with the Spir-it of

68

12286

74

12286

CONTRALTO SOLO.

And there were dwell-ing in Je - ru - sa - lem

Jews, de - vout men, from ev' - ry na-tion un-der

heav - - en; and when this

sound was heard, the mul - ti-tude came to - -

IN SOLOMON'S PORCH.

-geth - - -er, and were all a-mazed, and mar-velled.

Soprano.

Alto.

Tenor. THE PEOPLE.

Bass. Be-

CHORUS.

pp staccato

-hold, are not all these which

84

tongues the wonderful works of God!

hear them speak in our tongues.

We do hear them speak in our

We do hear them speak in our tongues the wonderful works of

86

What mean-eth

tongues the won-der-ful works of God!

God!

sonor.ᵉ

12286

-hold, are not all these which speak Ga-li-læ - ans?

What

What mean-eth this?

mean- -eth this?

And how hear we, ev-er-y man in our own

Ye men of Ju-dæ-a, and all ye that dwell at Je-

-ru-sa-lem, be this known____ un-to you, and give

ear_____ un--to____ my___ words: this is

that which was spoken____ by the prophet,____ "It shall come to pass____

dreams, and it shall be__ that who-so-ev-er__ shall call on the

name of the Lord, shall be sav- -ed."

Ye men of Israel, hear these words: __ Je-sus,

Je-sus of Na-zar-eth, a Man ap-prov-ed of God un-to you by

now see and hear. Let all the house of Is-rael

know as-sur-ed-ly, that God hath made Him both

Lord and Christ; This Je-sus, Whom ye cru-ci-fi-ed.

CONTRALTO SOLO.

Tenor. ("Daugh-

THE PEOPLE. ("His blood be on us, and on our

Bass. ("His blood be on us, and on our

CHORUS.

Spir - it of grace.

Of His own will, God brought us

Spir - it of grace.

Of His own

Of His own will, God brought us

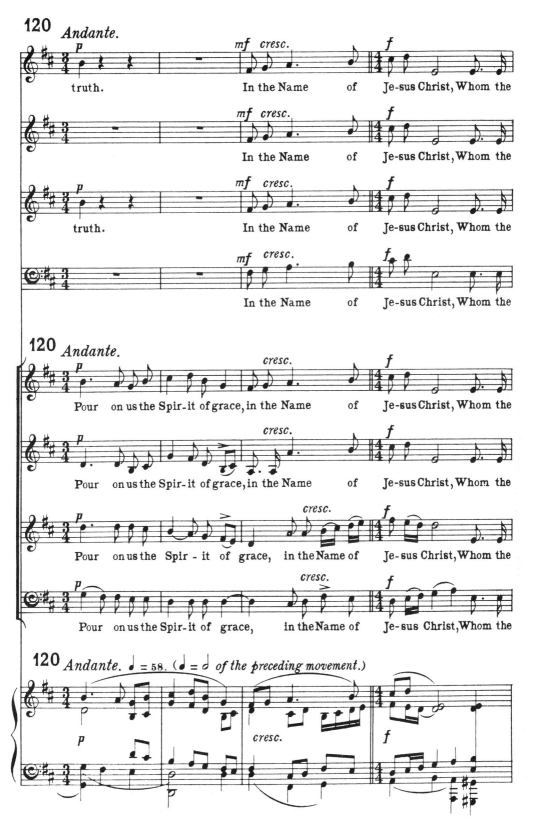

IV.
THE SIGN OF HEALING.
(AT THE BEAUTIFUL GATE.)

God!

God!

God!

God!

♩ = 120.

sfp —— *ff*

Ped. ✱

134 PETER. *f*

Ye men of Is-ra-el,—why mar-vel ye at this man?—

fp *pp*

f maestoso *cresc.*

—— The God of A-braham, of I-saac, and of

138 *a tempo* *espress.* *dim.* *pp*

-rise with heal - -ing_____ in His wings,_____

a tempo

with heal - -ing_____ in His

139 *pp* *f molto cantabile*

wings._____ Un - to you

ppp *mf*

first God,_____ hav - ing rais - ed up_____ His Ser - -

138

12286

THE ARREST.

And as they spake, the priests and the Sadducees came up-on them,

be - ing sore trou - bled, ___ be - cause they pro - claim - ed in

Je - sus ___ the re - sur - rec - tion ___ of the dead: and they laid

158

Who heal - eth all in - firm - - i - ties. The Gos - - - pel of the King - - dom,

sfp *cresc.* *f*

p *cresc.* *f* *allargando* *sf*

159 *Grandioso* *f*

a tempo ♩ = 72.

sfp

ffp

darkness; I me-di-tate on Thee; in the
night ___ Thy song shall be with me a prayer un-to the
God ___ of my life.

166 *molto lento*

pp colla parte

167 *a tempo, più lento*

pp rit.

rit.

a tempo, più lento

rall.

lunga.

dim.

pp

ppp

V.
THE UPPER ROOM.
IN FELLOWSHIP.

The rul - - ers gather to - geth - er against the Lord ___ and His An-

The rul - - ers gather to - geth - er against the Lord ___ and His An-

Lord, ___ behold their threat'n - - - ings.

Lord, ___ behold their threat'n - - ings.

- oint - ed: Lord, ___ behold their

- oint - ed:

M

THE BREAKING OF BREAD.

SOLI & CHORUS.

food and drink _____ and life e-ter-

food and drink _____ and life e-ter-

food and drink _____ and life e-ter-

food and drink _____ and life e-ter-

- nal _____ through Thy Ser- -vant.

- nal _____ through Thy Ser- -vant.

- nal _____ through Thy Ser- -vant.

- nal _____ through Thy Ser- -vant.

172

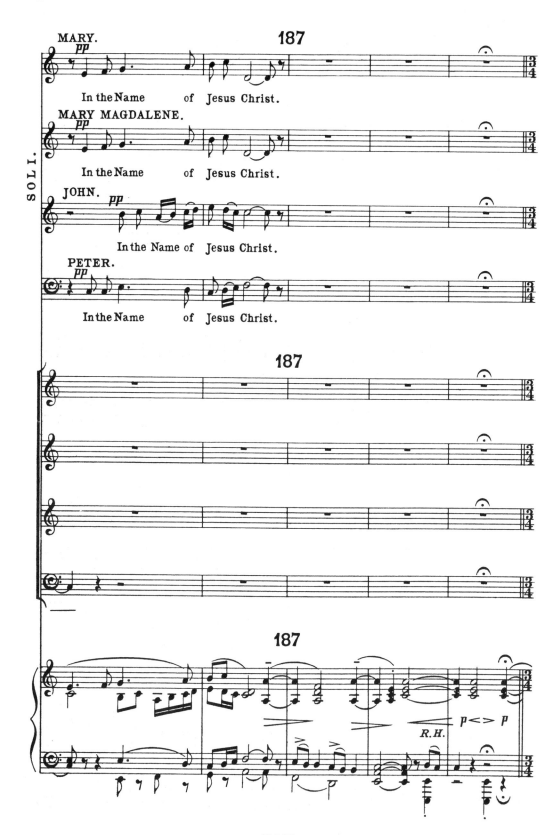

12286

THE PRAYERS.

188

Printed and bound in Great Britain by
Caligraving Limited Thetford Norfolk

6/97 (27951)

THE CHORAL MUSIC OF EDWARD ELGAR

THE APOSTLES
Oratorio for SATBB soli, chorus & orchestra

CARACTACUS
Cantata for STBarB soli, chorus & orchestra

THE DREAM OF GERONTIUS
Oratorio for M-S TB soli, chorus & orchestra

THE EARLY PART SONGS (1890-1891)
For SATB with divisions

FIVE UNACCOMPANIED PART-SONGS opus 71, 72 & 73
For SATB with divisions

FOUR LATIN MOTETS
For SATB & organ

FOUR UNACCOMPANIED PART-SONGS opus 53
For SATB with divisions

FROM THE GREEK ANTHOLOGY
Five unaccompanied part-songs for TTBB

GIVE UNTO THE LORD (PSALM 29)
For chorus & orchestra

GREAT IS THE LORD
For SATB chorus & organ or orchestra

THE KINGDOM
Oratorio for SATB soli, chorus & orchestra

THE LATER PART-SONGS (1902-1925)
For unaccompanied SATB with divisions

THE LIGHT OF LIFE (LUX CHRISTI)
Oratorio for SATB soli, chorus & orchestra

THE MUSIC MAKERS
Ode for contralto solo, chorus & orchestra

SEVEN ANTHEMS
For SATB (one for SA)

THE SPIRIT OF ENGLAND
For S or T Solo, chorus & orchestra

TE DEUM & BENEDICTUS IN F
For SATB chorus, orchestra & organ

THREE UNACCOMPANIED PART-SONGS
For SATB with divisions

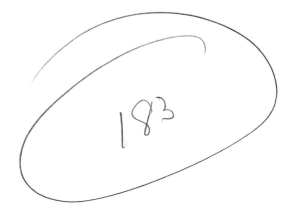

183

Const in Africa
a titter ran around
the room –
(Alan Hoff)

Titter ye not